EX CAMERA 1860 - 1960

PHOTOGRAPHS FROM THE COLLECTIONS OF THE NATIONAL LIBRARY OF IRELAND

COMPILED AND EDITED BY NOEL KISSANE

NATIONAL LIBRARY OF IRELAND, DUBLIN, 1990

PUBLISHED WITH ASSISTANCE FROM KODAK IRELAND LIMITED

ACKNOWLEDGEMENTS

The following individuals and institutions have contributed in various ways towards the compiling of this publication and an associated exhibition and are acknowledged with gratitude: Sgt Gregory Allen, Mr John A. Burgess, Marcus de Búrca, Uas., Mr Dermot Carlin, Mr Patrick Casey, Mr Edward Chandler, Mr Harold Clarke, Sister Catherine Codd, Principal, St Mary's College, Mountmellick; Mr Pat Cooke, Curator, the Pearse Museum; Mr Stephen Coonan, Mr Finbar Corry, Lt-Col Con Costello, Dr Maurice Craig, Mr Tom Cranitch, Professor Louis Cullen, Mr Liam Daly, Mr David Davison, Mr Joe Dealy, Pádraig de Barra, Uas., Mr Luke Dillon-Mahon, D.M. Prints, Ltd , Mr Pat Duffner, Mr Michael Duncan, Rev. Seán Farragher CSSp, Blackrock College; Ms Marie Farrell, Exhibition Centre, Castlebar; Fermanagh County Museum, Mr Clifton Flewitt, Mr John Graham, County Librarian, Co. Monaghan; Very Rev. Michael Green P.P., Kilkee; Mr Kieran Hickey, Ms Silvia Hopkins, National Army Museum, London; Mr Jim Kemmy, T.D., Mr John Kennedy, Capt. Percy W. Kennedy, Very Rev. Anthony King, Adm., Westport; Kodak Ireland Limited — Mr Declan Brennan, Ms Katrina McCarthy; Capt. Victor Lang, Military Archives, Cathal Brugha Barracks; Mr Pat Lavelle, Knock Shrine; Rt Rev. Msgr Mícheál Ledwith, President, St Patrick's College, Maynooth; Mr Denis McCarthy, Rev. Owen McEneaney, Mr Alf MacLochlainn, Mr Barry Mason, Mr John Moore, Keeper, Department of Transport, Ulster Folk and Transport Museum; Mrs Elizabeth Morgan, Mr George Morrison; National College of Art and Design — Mr Bill Bolger and Ms Linda King, Department of Visual Communications, for design of publication, exhibition and poster; National Museum of Ireland — Ms Mairead Dunlevy, Mr John Farrell who mounted the exhibition, Mr Michael Kenny, Dr Michael Ryan, Dr Patrick F. Wallace, Director; Ms Veronica Nicholson, Professor T.P. O'Neill, Aodh Ó Tuama, Uas., Curator, Cork Public Museum; Park Public Relations — Ms Leonie Brennan; Mr Rex Roberts, Mr Dick Roche, Mr John Roe; Royal Dublin Society — Dr Charles Mollan, Mr Michael Moloney; Mr Michael Ryan, Very Rev. Peter Scott P.P., Ballyheigue; Mr Robert N. Smart, Keeper, University of St Andrews; Mr C.P. Smith, Mr John Smyth, *The Munster Express,* Mr Glenn Thompson; Ulster Museum — Dr P.S. Doughty, Keeper of Geology, Mr Noel Nesbitt, Librarian, Department of Local History; Mr Peter Walsh, Curator, the Guinness Museum; Ms Anne Ward, County Librarian, Co. Louth; Mr Roger Weatherup, Curator, Armagh County Museum; Dr Kevin Whelan, Mrs Ita Wynne. Various members of the staff of the National Library have contributed, including Mr Dónal Begley, Chief Herald of Ireland, Ms Theresa Biggins, Mr Tom Desmond, Ms Laura Dillon, Mr John Lyons, Mr Philip McCann, Feargus Mac Giolla Easpaig, Uas., Dr Eilís Ní Dhuibhne, Dónall Ó Lúanaigh, Uas., Keeper of Printed Books, Mr Martin Ryan, and especially Mr Eugene Hogan, Photographer, and Mr Gerard Lyne who read and commented on the text.

First published in 1990 by the National Library of Ireland

©The National Library of Ireland

British Library Cataloguing in Publication Data:
National Library of Ireland
Ex camera 1860-1960: photographs from the collections of the National Library of Ireland

1. Photographs. Special subjects: Ireland. Catalogues, indexes

I. Title II. Kissane, Noel
779.994150474

ISBN 0 907328 16 4

Design by Linda King NCAD
Duotone separations: Colour Repro Ltd, Dublin
Typeset by Printset & Design Limited
Printed by Betaprint International Ltd, Dublin

CONTENTS

Front Cover: Amateur photographers at Clonbrock, Co. Galway, 1899. In the centre is Augusta, Lady Clonbrock; the others are her daughter, the Hon. Ethel Dillon; her sister-in-law, the Hon. Katherine Dillon; her son, the Hon. Robert Edward Dillon; and her daughter, the Hon. Edith Dillon (afterwards Lady Mahon). Robert Edward has a Kodak cartridge camera and the others have Kodak box cameras.
Clonbrock R.23358

Back Cover: Main Street, Rathdrum, Co. Wicklow, period 1910-20. The plaque on the house to the left represents the Cyclists' Touring Club. The motor car has an English registration; the passenger in front may be an R.I.C. man or possibly the chauffeur.
Eason 3922

Photographs evoke a sense of the past more potent than actual reportage. Their impact is immediate and crosses the barriers of language, age and educational abilities.

The National Library has a significant collection of photographs providing a unique record of the people and places of Ireland. Many of these are well-known, in particular the 40,000 glass-plate negatives which comprise the Lawrence Collection. This publication serves as an introduction to some of the other collections, and gives us a glimpse of the hidden delights to be found there. Many of the collections are, as yet, only partially catalogued. Valuable work on the Poole and Clonbrock collections is currently being undertaken by Dr Eilís Ní Dhuibhne, Assistant Keeper in charge of Prints, Drawings and Photographs.

Our plans for this fine storehouse of images include a conservation programme on the Lawrence Collection. We gratefully acknowledge the assistance of the National Lottery in this regard. Ultimately we would aim to catalogue and store these images on video-disc, thus providing our readers with ready visual access to this archive.

The National Library is fortunate in its friends, and we acknowledge in particular the financial assistance provided by Kodak Ireland Limited towards the publication of this book. We are also grateful to the Department of the Taoiseach who has generously provided funds to enable us to send an exhibition of this material on tour.

Dr Patricia Donlon, Director,
National Library of Ireland

Since its foundation in 1877 the National Library of Ireland has assembled an extensive collection of photographs of Irish interest. They have come from many different sources and represent the work of a great variety of photographers, both amateur and professional. Some of the items came in as solitary prints while others were acquired as groups mounted in albums. The National Library has also acquired a number of collections of photographic negatives in the medium of glass plates and sheet film. As might be expected, the coverage is limited for the decades immediately after the invention of photography which occurred in 1839, long before the National Library was established. However, one of the collections of glass-plate negatives, the Stereo Collection, dates back to around 1860 and from then onwards the coverage is fairly continuous up to the present day.

This publication is designed to show the range and variety of the National Library's holdings for the period for which they are most comprehensive and most interesting, that is from roughly 1860 to 1960. The photographs selected are for the most part typical of the collections and they are arranged in groups to illustrate various aspects of Ireland and Irish life over the period.

The majority of the items are from the major collections of negatives. These collections were created for a variety of reasons, each one over a period of years or a period of decades. Each represents a considerable achievement on the part of an individual, a family or a business concern.

The National Library of Ireland was founded in 1877 and the present building was opened on 29 August 1890.

Only one, that is the Lawrence Collection, has been the subject of detailed research and an adequate publication. They all deserve serious study and eventually each one should have a publication outlining its history and illustrating its nature and range of content. In the meantime the following brief descriptions may serve as introductions and enable the reader to understand the genesis and background of the individual items included in this publication.

1. The Stereo Collection

This consists of 3050 glass-plate negatives from the period c.1860-83. Each negative has twin images of the same subject, a left-eye view and a right-eye view, taken by a camera fitted with twin lenses. When the twin pictures were printed from the negative and viewed in a stereoscope, an apparatus with twin eye-pieces, they blended into a single picture which had a three-dimensional effect and an air of reality. From about 1850 many photographers used the stereoscopic technique to enhance their pictures and the stereoscope became a popular diversion in the drawing rooms of the middle and upper classes.

A stereoscope of the period 1860-80.

In Dublin, among the photographers who provided pictures for the stereoscope was James Simonton, whose business in Grafton Street was named the Royal Panopticon of Science and Art, and Frederick Holland Mares who created a comprehensive collection of Irish views. It seems that some of their negatives and those of a number of other photographers were acquired by John Fortune Lawrence, a dealer with a shop in Grafton Street known as the Civet Cat Bazaar which sold toys and fancy-goods

and included a photographic gallery. Eventually John Fortune's stock of stereo negatives passed to his more energetic brother, William Mervyn Lawrence, who had established the famous Lawrence photographic business in Sackville Street (now O'Connell Street) in 1865. William Lawrence proceeded to market stereo pictures from these and other negatives and his own photographers added to the range. The trade was mainly directed at tourists and people on holiday but there was also a strong local demand. So, as well as views of places like Killarney and the Giant's Causeway most cities and towns are represented in the collection. However, by the early 1880s the popular craze

A stereo camera being operated by Lord Dunlo, 1864. (Clonbrock R.23351)

for stereo views had declined and Lawrence largely abandoned that line of business. The collection of stereo negatives was withdrawn and kept in storage until 1943 when it was acquired by the National Library along with the main Lawrence Collection. The National Library has published a folder with 25 of the views and information on the collection under the title *Ireland 1860-80 from Stereo Photographs* (Dublin, 1981). In that publication and in this selection just one of the twin images is reproduced in each case.

2. The Lawrence Collection

This is the most important photographic collection in the National Library both by virtue of its range of content and the quality of the photography. It consists of 40,000 glass-plate negatives, mainly from the period 1880-1914 but including some items from as early as 1870. A detailed

William Mervyn Lawrence (1840-1932) and his wife Fanny Henrietta. Following an accident Lawrence had his right arm amputated, probably around the time he set up his business.

study of the firm of William Lawrence and the Lawrence Collection has been carried out by Kieran Hickey, whose findings, together with a selection of the photographs, were published under the title *The Light of Other Days* (London, 1973).

William Lawrence was not himself a photographer but he was an astute entrepreneur who recognised that photography was potentially a very profitable business. In 1865 he opened a photographic studio in his mother's toy and fancy-goods shop, which occupied a prime position almost opposite the General Post Office in Sackville Street. At the time there was great demand for studio portraits and from the start he employed a well-known portrait photographer. He was also well aware of the interest in stereo pictures and he took over the sale of these from his brother John Fortune. Next he became involved in the production side of this business and he acquired and printed from John Fortune's collection of negatives. By the late 1860s he had also organised the taking and production of single-image views. The business thrived and in addition to photographers Lawrence's employed a staff of printers, artists (colourists and retouchers) and sales personnel.

LAWRENCE'S GREAT BAZAAR & PHOTOGRAPHIC GALLERIES

5, 6, & 7, UPPER SACKVILLE-ST. DUBLIN.

A wet-plate photographer at work. (From Gaston Tissandier *History of Photography*, London, 1876).

The outdoor side of the business was hampered by the cumbersome wet-plate process in use at the time. The glass plates had to be prepared on site and after exposure they had to be developed at once in a portable darkroom. However, by 1880 the dry-plate process was available and photographers no longer had to transport so much awkward equipment. Cameras were now smaller and lighter, the dry plates needed no preparation and after exposure they could be taken back and developed in the more ideal conditions of the studio darkroom. It was providential for Lawrence's that just as the firm was adopting the new technology it had the services of a new chief photographer who exploited it to the full. This was the indefatigable Robert French who became chief photographer about 1880. French was born in Dublin and spent some years in the Royal Irish Constabulary before he joined Lawrence's. In his new career he worked his way up as printer, artist and assistant photographer. The business now specialised in marketing prints of various sizes, framed pictures, albums and lantern slides, for all of which French provided the original negatives. When required, he travelled down the country by train to take the photographs. He brought the negatives back to Dublin

and developed them. Views had to be up-to-date so he took photographs of the same scenes periodically. In all, French probably generated 30,000 negatives, that is three quarters of the collection.

Robert French (1841-1917) at the time of his retirement in 1914.

In the 1890s a new line of business developed when the Post Office allowed postcards to be sent without envelopes. This became a very profitable line especially after 1902 when one full side of the postcard could be devoted to a picture. Demand became overwhelming and Lawrence's had the facilities to provide a wide range of pictures. It had its cards printed in Germany, some in colour, and it became the major publisher of postcards in the country. Lawrence's cards were mostly topographical and the range of views included scenic spots, tourist attractions, cities and towns and, where there was sufficient demand, also many villages.

Lawrence's business prospered for the best part of fifty

years. However, in the second decade of this century it declined sharply. Among the contributory reasons was the fact that photographs had become extremely common as good reproductions were then appearing daily in newspapers and magazines. The current craze was for the cinema and moving pictures, and when people wanted 'snapshots' they could take their own with a 'box-brownie'. By that time both French and Lawrence were in their seventies; the former retired in 1914 and the latter in 1916. That same year during the Easter Rising the premises in Sackville Street were looted and burnt down. Most of the portrait negatives were destroyed but fortunately the negatives of the views were stored in Rathmines and survived. The firm finally closed down in 1942 and the following year the view negatives were acquired by the National Library.

Apart from the book *The Light of Other Days*, Kieran Hickey has used the photographs for a documentary film with the same title, and also for a film illustrating the Dublin of James Joyce's novel *Ulysses*. Many of the photographs have been reproduced in various other books and films and the collection is generally well-known.

3. The Clonbrock Collection

There are about 3,000 items in the collection and it includes glass-plate negatives, sheet-film negatives, lantern slides and some albums. It was created by various members of the family of Dillon, Barons Clonbrock, of Ahascragh, Co. Galway, during the period 1860-1930.

For much of the nineteenth century photography was generally carried out by professional photographers or members of the upper classes. Cameras and all the other equipment were expensive, and considerable time had to be devoted to preparing the wet-plates, developing the negatives and printing the photographs. As a result, only those with a fair measure of wealth and leisure tended to take up photography as a hobby. It became particularly fashionable with the landed gentry and a great deal of material in the way of prints and albums has come to the National Library from that source. In some cases collec-

tions of negatives have also survived. Among the more notable are the collection at Birr Castle, Co. Offaly, which was created by Mary, Countess of Rosse, and the Clonbrock Collection.

Many of the items in the Clonbrock Collection were taken by Luke Gerald Dillon, 4th Lord Clonbrock, and his wife Augusta, of the Crofton family of Mote Park, Co. Roscommon, both of whom were taking photographs for some years prior to their marriage in 1866. Their enthusiasm was such that they had a studio and darkroom built in the grounds at Clonbrock. The collection illustrates many aspects of life on a typical landed estate over a period of seventy years. As well as portraits and views of family and friends on festive and sporting occasions, the coverage also includes house-servants, farm-workers and tenants, and many of the local community activities with which members of the family were involved.

When Clonbrock was sold in 1976 the estate records and the photographic negatives and albums were acquired by the National Library.

Clonbrock in the period 1860-70.

4. The Poole Collection

This is a large collection of approximately 70,000 glass-plate negatives. It was generated by the family firm of A.H. Poole of 34 the Mall, Waterford, over the period 1884-1954. The firm operated mainly as commercial photographers and most of the photographs were commissioned by clients. In addition to Waterford city and the adjoining areas of the county, the business extended as far as New Ross and it also covered the southern areas of Co. Kilkenny.

In addition to the business at 34 the Mall, Poole's also had this premises at 134 the Quay, next-door to Reginald's Tower.

The firm's order books and indexes were acquired with the collection and these give the name of the client who commissioned each photograph, the date, and in some instances a note on the subject. Many of the items are group photographs of personnel in business firms, schools, clubs and societies. Also, there are occasional actuality photographs, some of which were published in newspapers at the time. The firm also published various series of postcards, some in colour, and they produced individualised postcards for local business firms and other institutions. The vast majority of the photographs are portraits and while these are not of general interest they may be of great significance for particular individuals.

Unfortunately it has not yet been possible to process and catalogue the collection as a whole. However, work is now in progress on the most important section of the collection, the series of whole-plate negatives. This amounts to 4,680 items, dating right through from 1884 to 1954. They are particularly valuable as generally the more important photographs were taken on whole-plate negatives. With one exception the Poole items included in this selection are from the whole-plate series.

5. The Eason Collection

Like a large part of the Lawrence Collection this was created to cater for the postcard trade. It is a relatively small collection, but it amounts to 4,090 glass-plate negatives and dates from about 1900 to the late 1930s. At the turn of the century the Dublin firm of Eason & Son Ltd was a large wholesale and retail business mainly involved in the book, newspaper and stationery trade. Postcards were among the lines it carried and as it had its own printing works it was relatively easy to extend into the production side of the business. Like Lawrence's it covered the whole island and concentrated on tourist attractions and holiday resorts. It did a good local trade as it had sales kiosks in most railway stations and it produced cards with topical views for these and other local outlets. Most of its cards were published under the imprint *Signal*, but it also produced individualised cards for a variety of customers including business firms and religious institutions.

The negatives were generated by a number of different photographers and some of them were provided by clients who required individualised postcards. A number are inscribed with the name 'Poulton' and others have the initials 'W.R.& S.' These relate to the London firm of Poulton & Son and the Edinburgh firm of William Ritchie & Sons, both of which published postcards. In the case of Poulton's it is probable that Eason's acquired a collection of their Irish negatives at some time. The 'W.R. & S.' negatives were probably generated by Eason's but were used by Ritchie's on occasion to produce editions of postcards aimed at the Irish immigrant market in Britain and Ritchie's inscribed their initials on them.

During the Rising in 1916 Eason's shop in Sackville Street suffered much the same fate as that of Lawrence's on the other side of the street and it was destroyed by fire. Fortunately, their negatives also were stored elsewhere — at the firm's printing works in Gloucester Place. The collection was acquired by the National Library some years after the printing side of the business closed down in 1941.

6. The Valentine Collection.
The well-known firm of Valentine & Sons of Dundee generated this collection for the postcard trade. It consists of 3,000 negatives, some on glass plates and some on sheet film. They cover the period from about 1903 to 1960. The content is much the same as that of the Eason Collection but the coverage does not include Northern Ireland. The negatives were generated mainly by Valentine's own staff of photographers. However, a number seem to have been purchased or commissioned from various other photographers, including Duffner Brothers of Dundalk. Many of the sheet-film negatives are copies cut to postcard-

size. In some cases the postcards were produced as photographic prints direct from the negative onto a roll of paper moving in 'stop-start' fashion. As the roll was developed it produced high-quality postcards in a reasonably fast, automated process.

In the late 1950s Valentine's began to phase out the production of monochrome postcards. Eventually through the agency of Duffner Brothers the National Library acquired the monochrome negatives relating to the Republic.

7. The Morgan Collection
The Morgan Collection differs from those already described in that it was created by one individual and consists almost entirely of aerial photographs. It has close on 3,000

Capt. A. C. Morgan DFC; he was killed at the age of thirty-eight when his plane crashed near Shannon Airport in January 1958.
(Irish Independent)

sheet-film negatives from the period 1954-57 and it includes items from most counties in the Republic and a number from Northern Ireland. The photographs were taken by the late Capt. Alexander Campbell Morgan, trading as Aerophotos. Some of the locations were selected on a speculative basis but many of the photographs were commissioned. The list of clients includes newspapers, industrial concerns, schools and churches. A number of the photographs were published by the *Irish Independent* in a weekly series in 1957. The photographer's catalogue was acquired with the collection and gives the location and date of each item.

8. The Keogh Collection

This small collection of 230 glass-plate negatives dates from the period 1914-23. It was generated by the firm of Keogh Brothers of Lower Dorset Street, Dublin. It includes actuality pictures of incidents during the 1916 Rising, the 1917 elections and the Civil War. It also includes a large number of portraits of personalities of the time. Although it is a relatively small collection it is well known and some of the items have been published many times over the years.

9. Albums and other collections

A number of the photographs in this selection were acquired as individual items and some were acquired in collections of prints or in albums. It is not practical to outline the genesis of all of them but the following are especially important:

a. The earliest is *Wynne's Souvenir Scrap Album of Mayo, Galway and the Western Highlands*. It contains 140 prints mounted-in, most of which are from the early 1870s. They include urban and rural scenes and some actuality pictures of political meetings and community activities. The photographs were taken by Thomas J. Wynne who had a thriving photographic business and a newsagency and stationery shop in Castlebar. Later his sons had branches of the business in Loughrea, Tipperary and Portarlington. At the time various firms of photographers issued albums of mounted-in photographs.

b. Three items in this selection are from *Ireland through the Stereoscope*. This is a boxed collection of 100 stereo pictures published by Underwood & Underwood, New York, *c.*1905.

c. The Congested Districts Board Collection consists of 105 prints relating to the work of the Board which was established in 1891 to promote development in the counties along the west coast. Many of the items are by the Belfast photographer Robert J. Welch whom the Board commissioned for some work in June 1914. Annotations in his hand appear on his prints. The negatives of some of the prints are in the Welch Collection in the Ulster Museum but not those of the items reproduced in this publication.

d. The final item to be mentioned here is an album with forty photographs from the period May-July 1922. Most of the photographs are of Free State forces on active service in Dublin and Limerick. They appear to have been taken with official sanction and some are stamped 'passed by censor.' It was acquired from Mr A.E. Fitzelle and is now designated 'Fitzelle Album'.

In the text following each photograph the source reference includes the name of the collection or album except in the case of items acquired as individual prints where only the reference number is given.

Kilkenny in the period 1860-80. On the skyline to the left is the Black Abbey Dominican Church. The Black Abbey was a Dominican friary founded in 1225 by William the Marshall, Strongbow's son-in-law. The present structure is mainly an eighteenth-century restoration of the original church. To the right is the Roman Catholic St Mary's Cathedral which was completed in 1857.

Stereo P.1215

Scotch Street, Armagh, with St Patrick's Church of Ireland
Cathedral in the distance, *c.*1880. The cathedral was rebuilt
in 1261-68 by Archbishop Ó Scanaill on the site of St
Patrick's principal church. It has been repaired, modified
and restored over the centuries and in effect the building
now dates for the most part from the 1830s.
Stereo P.2160

O'Connell Bridge, Dublin, shortly after the Winged Victories were added to the base of the O'Connell Monument in 1883. The statue in the foreground is of William Smith O'Brien, the Young Ireland leader. It has since been moved across the bridge to a position between the O'Connell Monument and the statue of Sir John Grey, proprietor of the *Freeman's Journal*, which is prominent in white in this photograph. The horse trams were introduced in 1875.

Stereo P.2702

Cruises Royal Hotel, Limerick, period 1890-1910. The
omnibus at the door belonged to the hotel and was used
for carrying guests to and from the railway station.
Lawrence I.3423

High Street, Belfast, in the period 1906-09. In Belfast electric trams replaced the horse trams in 1905. The style of tram featured here with the top deck open to the elements was replaced in 1910 by the more practical model with the top deck enclosed.

The clock tower in the distance is the Albert Memorial which was erected in 1869 in tribute to Queen Victoria's late Prince Consort.
Eason 417

PATRICK STREET AND HILL, CORK.

Patrick Street, Cork, in the late 1930s. Most of the cars are
Fords, to some extent due to the fact that they were
assembled locally. Buses were providing public transport at
this period, replacing the tram system which closed down
in 1931.

Valentine R.880

EYRE SQUARE, SHOWING ANCIENT GATEWAY, GALWAY.

Eyre Square, Galway, c.1938-39. The cars in the foreground are an Austin, a Standard (ZC 2964), a Ford with a wheel jacked up and a Hillman; the two in front of the Standard are Fords.

The monument on the left illustrates a Continental style of architecture once common in Galway. It consists of a doorway and window from the mansion of Martin Browne erected in Lower Abbeygate Street c.1627. It was moved to this site as an entrance to Eyre Square in 1905-06.
Valentine R.1735

O'Connell Bridge, Dublin, *c.*1938-39. The motor cars in the
foreground are taxis. The vehicle on Bachelor's Walk is a
Lucan tram and a bus is pulling out from Eden Quay.
Valentine R.1429

Derry, the Foyle and Craigavon Bridge, July 1955. The Waterside district is across the Foyle on the left. St Columb's Cathedral is on the near side in a line with Craigavon Bridge. Further to the right a section of the town wall extends down to the far side of the open ground. The Bogside district begins outside the wall at this point and extends away to the right beyond the picture. *Morgan* 1392

O'Connell Street, Dublin, from the top of Nelson's Pillar,
in the period 1957-59. The Pillar was demolished in 1966.
Valentine R.5140

The Slaney and Enniscorthy, Co. Wexford, period 1860-80.
In the background is Vinegar Hill with the stump of the
windmill where the insurgents had their command post in
1798.
Stereo P.1535

Charlestown, Co. Mayo, in the early 1870s. The town was built during the Famine by Charles Strickland, agent for Charles Henry, 14th Viscount Dillon. It was originally named Newtown Dillon, but Charlestown was used as an alternative from the 1860s, in honour of Strickland or of Dillon or possibly both. There are two weighbridges, each with a shelter for the attendant. In market towns they were necessary for weighing items of produce. A percentage of the value was paid as a toll, in that period usually to the local landlord.

Wynne Album R.22472

Ahascragh, Co. Galway, *c.*1902. The two men in uniform
are members of the Royal Irish Constabulary. They may
be watching cleaning-up operations after a fair—at the time
the village had four fairs a year.
Clonbrock R.23352

Enniskillen, Co. Fermanagh, c.1905. Apart from the man on the left the figures in the foreground are soldiers of the Royal Inniskilling Fusiliers relaxing beside the Military Hospital. The dark figures are dressed in scarlet and the others are wearing hospital uniforms.
Ireland through the Steroscope R.23169

The railway station, Abbeyleix, Co. Laois, *c.*1905. The
station was on the Portlaoise to Kilkenny line operated by
the Great Southern & Western Railway.
Eason 2654

O'Connell Street, Sligo, in the period 1910-20.
Eason 3391

Donegal Town, September 1954. The name *Dún na nGall*—Fort of the Foreigners—dates from Viking times. In the later middle ages Donegal was the seat of the O'Donnells, Kings of Tír Chonaill. The layout of the centre of the town with the Diamond as the focal point dates from the seventeenth century, when it was planned—and planted—by Sir Basil Brooke. The obelisk in the centre of the Diamond is a memorial to the Four Masters. The church behind it is that of the Church of Ireland. To the left of the church are the ruins of Donegal Castle, part of which was built by the O'Donnells in the sixteenth century.

Morgan 584

MAIN STREET, BALLINAMORE, CO. LEITRIM V R.8373.

Main Street, Ballinamore, Co. Leitrim, in the late 1950s.
The Morris Minor car has a Co. Leitrim registration (IT
3721) issued in January 1956. The registration of the van in
front (RR 11) was issued in Dublin in May 1955.
Valentine R.8373

West Street, Drogheda, Co. Louth, c. 1959-60. The cars are typical of the period. On the extreme left are a Skoda (Czechoslovakian) and a Ford; a Sunbeam-Talbot is in the middle of the road; those on the right are a Morris, a Ford and a Morris.
On the left is St Peter's Church where the embalmed head of St Oliver Plunkett is preserved. At the top of the street is the Tholsel which was built in 1770. It was used for meetings of the Corporation and as a courthouse; it is now a branch of the Bank of Ireland.
Valentine R.8413

Boatmen at Ross Castle, Killarney, Co. Kerry, period
1860-70.
Stereo P.83

Panorama of North County Louth and Carlingford Lough, period 1860-80. The photograph was taken from Flagstaff Hill on the northern side of the Carlingford range of mountains about nine miles from Dundalk. Towards the left, across the Border in Co. Down, is the sixteenth-century Narrow Water Castle at the point where the broad Newry River narrows on its way down to Carlingford Lough. The Mountains of Mourne are in the distance.
Stereo P.2139

The harbour at Ballintoy on the North Antrim coast
between Ballycastle and Bushmills, period 1860-80. Heaps
of chalk from nearby quarries are waiting to be shipped,
probably to Scotland for use in iron-smelting.
Stereo P.2267

Drawing home the corn. This item is from an album of
photographs relating to the Dun Laoire and South County
Dublin area in the period 1900-1910.
Dixon-Yeates Album R.22415

The Grand Canal near Naas, Co. Kildare, *c.*1910. The
vessel is a cargo steamer operated by the Grand Canal
Company.
Valentine 54137

Rundale plots at Lisaniska, near Castlebar, Co. Mayo, 1914. Rundale was a tradition in parts of the West of Ireland under which a group of smallholders held a tract of land as joint tenants. In the interests of equity each held a proportion of the better land and a proportion of the poorer land. Unfortunately each person's allocation was in the form of a number of unfenced and generally scattered plots.

This and the following item were taken by the Belfast photographer Robert J. Welch for the Congested Districts Board. Welch annotated this print: 'Each of the unfenced strips on hill-side is in the possession of a different tenant'. *Congested Districts Board* R.17597

A new concrete-block house at Ryehill, Monivea, Co.
Galway, constructed by the Congested Districts Board for
John Commons, 1914. The Board had acquired a large tract
of land at Ryehill which it divided into viable farms. These
were allocated to Commons and a number of other
smallholders who were migrated from congested districts.
Congested Districts Board R.17599

Harvesting turf at Annaverna Bog, north of Dundalk, Co. Louth, in the late 1940s. The men are 'footing' the turf, that is standing the partly dry sods in piles of seven or eight to dry them out thoroughly. Many Dundalk people cut turf at Annaverna and it provided them with cheap fuel every year.
Valentine R.8428

The two-day World Ploughing Championships for the Esso
Golden Plough at Killarney, Co. Kerry, 8 October 1954.
The competitors represented a total of twelve countries
including Canada and the United States. The individual
winner was Hugh Barr, a twenty-eight-year-old farmer from
Coleraine, Co. Derry.
Morgan 595

Bridget Sweeney and Mary Burke at the Gap of Dunloe, Killarney, Co. Kerry, period 1860-70. These photographs are in a series of seven items labelled 'Gap Girls' in the Stereo Collection. The girls sold liquid refreshments to tourists around Killarney. They are all pictured in the traditional dress of the locality. Bridget is wearing a Paisley shawl and a lined decorative skirt which is tucked up for greater mobility, exposing her petticoat. Mary is wearing a woollen shawl over a decorative neck-scarf. She has a white apron covering her red petticoat.
Stereo P.2852 & 2857

Women at St Senan's Well, Kilkee, Co. Clare, period 1860-70. The well is within the well-house which is a modern structure erected to keep cattle away. The water flows out along a gullet, sections of which are covered with flag-stones. The local people used the water for domestic purposes and the women did the washing downstream from the point where drinking water was taken.
The standing-stone on the left is supposed to have been thrown by St Senan at a time of drought with the promise that water would flow from the place where it landed.
Stereo P.1658

The photographer Thomas J. Wynne in his shop window at Main Street, Castlebar, Co. Mayo, Thursday, 26 October 1871. It is probable that Wynne made sure that the calendar in the window was displaying the correct date. Presumably the Blackwood's advertisement was for the following year's diaries.
Wynne Album R.22468

The donkey export trade at Waterford 1897. Here the
donkeys are being driven from the railway station to the
docks.
Poole W.P.822

Blacksmiths and stable-hands at the Dublin coal merchants,
Tedcastle, M'Cormick & Company, c.1905. The company
delivered coal by horse and cart and maintained a
considerable stable.
R.17915

Stall outside a Roman Catholic church during a mission, period 1905-10. Since the middle of the nineteenth century it was customary for Catholic churches to have a mission or retreat for one or two weeks every five years to promote the spiritual life of the community. The mission was conducted by priests from one of the 'preaching' orders, often the Redemptorists. Commercial traders took advantage of the attendant renewal of religious fervour to sell items such as medals and rosary beads from travelling stalls.

Eason 4070

The opening of the labour exchange, Waterford, 3 March 1910. Legislation enacted the previous year empowered the Board of Trade to establish labour exchanges 'to provide information as to employers requiring workpeople and workpeople seeking engagement.'
Poole W.P.2033

FISHERS AT WORK (WITH NETS) LOUGH NEAGH, ANTRIM.

Pollan fishermen at Lough Neagh, Co. Antrim, period 1910-20. The pollan is a freshwater herring which is also found in Lough Erne and Lough Derg. Pollan fishing was formerly the major industry on Lough Neagh but it has almost died out due to declining stocks.

The man on the left is emptying his net and the other man is checking a net. The woman is a hawker and she is putting fish into a basket which is partly obscured by a tin bath.

Eason 265

The crew of the Wexford lifeboat *John Stephens*. On the night of 22 February 1914 the Norwegian ship *Mexico* ran aground on the Keeragh Rock about five miles out from Fethard. The Fethard lifeboat went to the rescue but sank in heavy seas. Nine of the lifeboat crew and one of the *Mexico* crew perished. The *John Stephens* and other vessels eventually brought the survivors ashore.
Poole W.P.2537

The staff at Anderson & Scanlon's grocery shop, 104
Upper George's Street, Dun Laoire, Co. Dublin, period
1915-17.
R.22399

Effigy of Judge William Keogh, Castlebar, Co. Mayo, June 1872. Keogh was born in Galway and brought up as a Roman Catholic. As M.P. for Athlone he promoted nationalist policies but afterwards he took government office and eventually became a judge. In 1872 he was judge at a trial arising from a disputed election in Co. Galway and he denounced the Catholic bishops and clergy for their role in the election. As a result he was burnt in effigy at several towns around the country.

Wynne Album R.22471

The house of the widow McNamara, Bodyke, Co. Clare, June 1887. During the Plan of Campaign tenants on part of Colonel O'Callaghan's estate at Bodyke withheld their rents and 28 families were evicted, including eighty-year-old Mrs McNamara, her three sons and two daughters. The tenants were supported by the local clergy, two of whom appear in the photograph.
Lawrence Elbana 2662

Work in progress at the building of New Tipperary. In 1889 during the Plan of Campaign the people of Tipperary town stopped paying ground rents to their landlord, A.H. Smith-Barry. They proceeded to build a new town nearby on other property. Over £50,000 was spent on the work but with the 'Parnell Split' after November 1890 the country lost interest and no more money was provided. The townspeople had to abandon the project and make a settlement with Smith-Barry who had the new town levelled.
Lawrence R.2573

Police escorting farmers and their pigs to a bacon factory in Waterford, January 1897. In 1892 the factories began to purchase pigs direct from farmers, by-passing the professional pig buyers who had traditionally acted as middlemen. The Waterford pig buyers were a closely-knit group, most of whom lived in the Ballybricken area, and they carried on a campaign to recover their role in the trade. Here they were attempting to buy all pigs entering the city and farmers who refused to sell had to be escorted by police. To the right of centre a District Inspector with silver mountings on his shoulder belt is speaking to the policeman who is pointing towards the camera.
Poole W.P.770

The Lord Chief Justice, Sir Peter O'Brien, leaving the Imperial Hotel, Waterford, on his way to the Courthouse, 13 March 1897. The Lord Chief Justice was in Waterford as a special commissioner for the trial of a number of pig-buyers charged with crimes arising from their dispute with the bacon factories. The escort includes Hussars and four constables of the mounted section of the Royal Irish Constabulary. O'Brien was nicknamed 'Peter the Packer' due to the allegation that he 'packed' the juries when he acted as Crown Counsel at the Land League trials in Dublin in 1881-82.

Poole W.P.787

Fr Mathew's Boys' Brigade, Waterford, setting out for the commemoration of the Battle of Ross, Sunday, 28 May 1898. The *Waterford News* reported that 230 members of the Boys' Brigade bearing miniature pikes marched from the Temperance Hall in Parnell Street to the Quay, 'where they paraded for the purpose of being photographed by Messrs. Poole.' They were accompanied by a number of other groups including the Emmet Fife and Drum Band and they all travelled to New Ross by steamer.
Poole W.P.955

The 8th King's Royal Irish Hussars at Newbridge Barracks, Co. Kildare, period 1914-21. The troop stables appear to be relatively late structures built on the outside of the barrack square which is in the background.
Eason 2523

Parliament Street, Kilkenny, 10 August 1917. The occasion was the by-election at which the Sinn Féin candidate W.T. Cosgrave was elected. Polling took place at the Courthouse which is obscured by Power Brothers' premises. The old man in the foreground is wearing what appears to be a service medal. The gateway on the right leading to the New Market has since been removed.
Keogh 145

Children playing soldiers outside the Four Courts, Dublin, 15 April, 1922. Republican forces under the command of Rory O'Connor occupied the Four Courts on the night of 14 April. They fortified the building and in this photograph sandbags can be seen in position inside the gates. The Free State forces opened fire on 28 June and the garrison surrendered two days later.
Fitzelle Album R.22403

A Rolls-Royce armoured car in Lower Baggot Street, Dublin, June 1922. This was one of a number of vehicles which the Free State inherited from the British. It is displaying the Tricolour and the emblem of the Irish Defence Forces (*FF* i.e. *Fianna Fáil* in Sunburst). It was named 'The Big Fella' in honour of Michael Collins. The photograph was probably taken on 26 June following an attempt by Republican forces under Comdt Leo Henderson to commandeer vehicles from Ferguson's Garage. According to the *Irish Independent*, 'Dáil troops arrived promptly on the spot and surprised the raiding party'.

Fitzelle Album R.22406

The Drumreilly Upper Fife and Drum Band from Co. Leitrim, commemorating the 150th anniversary of the Battle of Ballinamuck, Co. Longford, on Sunday, 19 September 1948. Among the attendance at Ballinamuck was the President of Ireland, Mr. Seán T. O'Kelly, the Minister for External Affairs, Mr. Seán MacBride, and the Minister for Justice, General Seán MacEoin, who recalled that he had helped to organise the Drumreilly Upper Band many years before.

On the right is a unit of the Fórsa Cosanta Áitiúil (Local Defence Force) commanded by an officer of the regular army.

Valentine R.8380

Bellamont Forest, Cootehill, Co. Cavan, c.1869-70. The house was built c.1730 by Thomas Coote, Lord Justice of the King's Bench in Ireland. It was designed by his nephew Sir Edward Lovett Pearce. The original name was Coote Hill but it was changed to Bellamont Forest when Thomas Coote's grandson became Earl of Bellamont in 1767.

At the time of the photograph the Bellamont Forest estate amounted to 5,300 acres and the proprietor was Richard Coote. The photograph is in an album inscribed 'Lady Dartrey from Richard Coote, Bellamont Forest, 13 September 1870'.
Bellamont Forest Album R.22380

Coursefield, Claremorris, Co. Mayo, in the early 1870s. At
the time Coursefield was the residence of John Tighe, a
landlord with a small estate of about 400 acres.
Wynne Album R.22473

The Hon. Robert Edward Dillon (1869-1926), afterwards
5th Lord Clonbrock, and his sister, the Hon. Georgiana
Caroline Dillon, at Clonbrock, Co. Galway, c.1883.
Clonbrock R.23350

Gentry outside the Shell Cottage, Carton, Maynooth, Co. Kildare, period 1880-90. Carton was the seat of the Fitzgeralds, Dukes of Leinster. The Shell Cottage was an eighteenth-century house which was reconstructed as a secluded retreat by Charlotte Augusta, the 3rd Duchess, who died in 1859. The interior was lavishly decorated with rare shells, the collecting of which was a hobby fashionable among 'ladies of quality' at the time.
Lawrence R.390

Henry de la Poer Beresford, Marquess of Waterford, and his bride, Beatrice Frances Petty-Fitzmaurice, daughter of the Marquess of Lansdowne, being welcomed by the staff at his ancestral home, Curraghmore, Portlaw, Co. Waterford, following their marriage in London on 16 October 1887. The Prince of Wales attended the wedding which the *Waterford Mail* described as 'the most important and brilliant social function of the season'.

The couple had six children. In 1911 when he was aged thirty-six Lord Waterford was accidentally drowned at Curraghmore.

Poole W.P.900

A shooting party at Clonbrock, Co. Galway, period 1895-1900. Included are Luke Gerald, 4th Lord Clonbrock, on the extreme left; his wife Augusta at the back holding a plate-holder; her nephew, Capt. Arthur Crofton (afterwards Lord Crofton), is standing to her right; Lord Ardilaun is the other man at the back; one of the young men in front is the Hon. Robert Edward Dillon, son of Lord and Lady Clonbrock.
Clonbrock R.23359

Hay-making on the Clonbrock demesne, Ahascragh, Co.
Galway, *c.*1900. Most of the agricultural land on estates was
let to tenants but landlords usually farmed the demesne
around the residence through the agency of a steward.
Here, Lord Clonbrock's appropriately-named steward
Willie Hay is directing operations.
Clonbrock R.23356

Washing operations in the stable yard at Rockingham, Boyle, Co. Roscommon, period 1901-03. The vehicles involved are a family omnibus and a Panhard motor car with a wheel jacked up. The circular flagged area has a drain around the edge to take the water. The man in uniform is probably an R.I.C. officer and the two men on the right may be the head stable-man and the estate manager.

Rockingham was the centre of an estate of 29,000 acres. At this time the proprietor was Edward Charles Stafford-King-Harman, a minor. The house was burned down in 1957 but the demesne is now a public park.

Lawrence R.7331

The annual show of the Clonbrock and Castlegar
Cooperative Poultry Society at Clonbrock, Co. Galway,
1902. The Society was founded by Augusta, Lady
Clonbrock, in 1898 to promote poultry keeping in the area
and to ensure that the local women got reasonable prices
for their produce.
Clonbrock R.23348

Two titled gentlemen being photographed while attending the Oireachtas at Killarney in 1914. William Gibson, 2nd Baron Ashbourne (in kilt), was afterwards President of the Gaelic League. His companion, Valentine Patrick MacSwiney of Mashanaglass, Fermoy, Co. Cork, was descended from an illustrious Irish family and was created Marquis MacSwiney by Pope Leo XIII.

The photographer is using a ferrotype camera. It produced an image on a metal plate which was processed in the apparatus attached to the leg of the tripod under the photographer's left arm.

R.22390

Lady and Lord Talbot de Malahide and a Mrs Ryan with Irish Wolfhounds at Malahide Castle, Co. Dublin, 25 August 1928. The Talbots settled in Malahide at the time of the Anglo-Norman conquest and held the property continuously until the 1970s. The castle is for the most part post-medieval. The castle and grounds are now administered by Dublin Tourism and are open to the public.
R.22397

Undergraduate seminarians at St Patrick's College,
Maynooth, Co. Kildare, *c.*1880. The College was founded
by the Irish Parliament in 1795 as a seminary for clerical
students and as a place of higher education for lay students.
However, at this time it was reserved for clerical students.
Stereo P.1572

Teachers and pupils at Derrycreagh National School near
Glengarriff, Co. Cork, May 1899.
R.22395

Miss Crowe and Mr Gildea with their pupils at Kilglass
National School, Ahascragh, Co. Galway, *c*.1902. The girls
are in white pinafores. Some of the small boys on the left
who have not yet been breeched are also in pinafores.
The school was set up and run by Lord Clonbrock before
the national school system was established. It eventually
became a national school.
Clonbrock R.23360

Mr Andrew Carnegie laying the foundation stone of the new Waterford Free Library at Lady Lane, 19 October 1903. Among the attendance was the Librarian, John J. Morrin, also the Lord Mayor, the Town Clerk and members of the borough staff, all in full-dress uniform. Andrew Carnegie (1835-1919) was born in Scotland in humble circumstances. His parents took him to the United States where he became an extremely successful business entrepreneur with interests in railways, iron and steel. In 1901 he retired to Scotland and devoted himself to philanthropic work especially the provision of library premises.
Poole W.P.1313

Balladian National School, Co. Monaghan, *c.*1903. The teacher is standing at the door and the tall girl on the left may be a monitor, that is a pupil-teacher. The school was in existence at least as early as 1834 when it was run by a local committee. It later became a national school.
Ireland through the Stereoscope R.23168

An art class at Blackrock College, Co. Dublin, period 1904-08. The priest is Fr John Martin Ebenrecht CSSp, a native of Alsace. He was art teacher, bursar and architect at Blackrock and designed the new art room which was opened in 1904.

The photograph is in the form of a lantern slide mounted by Thomas H. Mason & Sons of Dame Street. Mason's were professional photographers but they also prepared lantern slides from photographs supplied by clients. The photograph may have been taken by Fr Hugh O'Toole CSSp, who was a photography enthusiast on the staff of the College at the time.

R.23184

Girls at gym class at the Ursuline Convent School,
Waterford, 3 April 1908.
Poole W.P.1796

St Columb's College, Derry, June 1955. This is a voluntary grammar school managed by the Diocese of Derry. At the time of the photograph it catered for boarders and day pupils.

The church which occupies a central position at the front of the main block is on the site of the Casino built in the eighteenth century by Frederick Hervey, Earl of Bristol and Bishop of Derry. The college museum, the two-storey building on the left, was modelled on the Casino.

Morgan 1388

The recreation grounds at St Mary's College, Mountmellick, Co. Laois, in the mid-1950s. St Mary's is run by the Presentation Sisters and was then an 'all Irish' boarding school for girls with an enrolment of 320. Students came from all over the country and there was great inter-county rivalry. Recreation was from 4.00 to 5.00 p.m. and the pupils walked around in groups of up to four. Reflecting the changes in the educational system in recent decades, St Mary's is now a mixed day-school catering for boys and girls from the locality.
Valentine R.8367

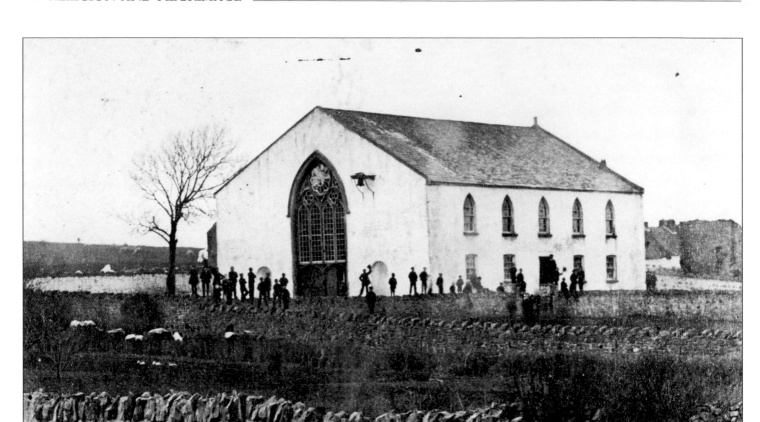

The Roman Catholic Church, Castlebar, Co. Mayo, in the early 1870s. It was built in 1801 and at the time of this photograph was described as 'a ramshackle building which has long outlived its time.' A replacement church was begun but for various reasons it was never completed. In the 1890s both the proposed replacement and the old church were demolished and the present church was built in 1901.
Wynne Album R.22470

St Mullin's, Co. Carlow, period 1890-1910. *Teach Mo-Ling* (Moling's House) was the principal foundation of the seventh century St Mo-Ling, a patron of South Leinster. The medieval ruins include walls of a nave-and-chancel church (beside the modern church) and the stump of a Round Tower. It was an important place of pilgrimage in the middle ages and the kings of South Leinster were buried there.

The photographer Robert French left his hat and coat in the jaunting car which he had probably hired in New Ross. He often included a jaunting car to give the picture some life and sometimes to indicate scale.

Lawrence I.825

Friars' Walk, Dominican College, Tallaght, Co. Dublin,
period 1890-1910. The College was established in 1855 as a
novitiate and house of studies. The Dominicans first
established foundations in Ireland at Dublin and Drogheda
in 1224.
Lawrence R.1133

Pilgrims at St Patrick's Cross, Station Island, Lough Derg, Co. Donegal, 1905. This medieval cross was damaged in the seventeenth century and only the shaft remains. The women have their heads covered as was customary on religious occasions up until the 1960s. All the pilgrims are barefoot.

Lough Derg became internationally famous in the later Middle Ages as the site of St Patrick's Purgatory, where the saint was said to have fasted for forty days and to have seen purgatory and hell.
Ireland through the Stereoscope R.23167

John Charles McQuaid, Archbishop of Dublin, inspecting a
Captain's Guard of Honour of men drawn from the 5th
Infantry Battalion, 1941. The occasion was possibly the
opening of the new church at St Bricin's Military Hospital,
Infirmary Road, Dublin, on 19 March that year.
R.22389

Guard of honour at a wedding at St Connell's Church, Glenties, Co. Donegal, 1941. The guard of honour was provided by the Local Security Force of which the bridegroom was the Assistant District Leader. The Force was established in May 1940 as an auxiliary during the Emergency. The 'B Group' of the Force was unarmed and performed auxiliary police duties. The 'A Group' (shown here) was armed and was reconstituted as the Local Defence Force at around the time of the photograph.
R.22387

PILGRIMS AT THE FOOT OF CROAGHPATRICK 11

Pilgrims at the foot of Croagh Patrick, Co. Mayo, in the early 1950s. The last Sunday of July has been the traditional day of pilgrimage to the top of the Reek where St Patrick is supposed to have fasted for forty days and forty nights. The statue of St Patrick was erected in this century.
Valentine R.8480

MASS AT THE GROTTO, BALLYHEIGUE.

Mass on pattern day at Our Lady's Well, Ballyheigue, Co. Kerry, in the 1950s. The pattern (i.e. patron) day was celebrated each year on 8 September, the birthday of the Virgin Mary. The well and its patron have been venerated for many centuries. The grotto is a relatively modern structure and the statue is of Our Lady of Lourdes.
Valentine R.8322

The annual blessing of the Aer Lingus fleet at Dublin Airport, 13 June 1954. Usually a representative selection of the planes was blessed and here there are four Bristol Wayfarers, two DC3s and a Vickers Viscount. The registration numbers were issued by the Department of Industry and Commerce and the letters EI designated the Republic of Ireland.

Morgan 102

Knock, Co. Mayo, August 1954. An apparition of the Virgin Mary accompanied by St Joseph and St John the Evangelist was reported to have taken place at the gable of Knock church on 21 August 1879. As a result the place has become a major centre of pilgrimage.

The photograph shows the original church with some additions. The gable is facing the camera. In 1940 an oratory with sliding glass doors was erected against it so that the ceremonies could take place in sight of the large outdoor congregation. In 1976 a basilica was erected to the right just beyond the edge of the photograph.
Morgan 428

Shooting seals, possibly on Achill Island, Co. Mayo, period 1860-80. In the west of Ireland people generally did not harm seals as they believed that they were reincarnated souls of the dead. However, some visitors shot them for sport.
Stereo P.1522

Members of the family of Dillon, Barons Clonbrock, and
friends playing croquet at Clonbrock, Co. Galway, *c.*1865.
Croquet was a sport popular with the gentry in the second
half of the nineteenth century.
Clonbrock R.23349

Mr T. Doyle, Yoletown Roller Mills, New Ross, Co. Wexford, with 'penny-farthing', November 1891. The 'spoon' brake, operated by hand, exerted pressure on the solid tyre. The photograph was taken in Poole's studio in front of a painted backdrop.
Poole X.5977

Polo at Dundalk, Co. Louth, period 1880-90. It was played
just outside the town on the demesne which was part of
the estate of the Earl of Roden.
Lawrence C.7579

HOTEL. GREENORE.   W L.

Tennis at the Greenore Hotel, Greenore, Co. Louth,
period 1900-10. The hotel was the property of the London
and North Western Railway. Among the flags and ensigns
are the Union Jack and the Naval Jack. At the time
Greenore was a thriving tourist resort.
Lawrence N.S.8305

A meeting of the West Carbery Foxhounds in West Cork. The occasion is St Patrick's Day, 1902. The Master is the writer Edith Somerville who is riding side-saddle on her white horse Bridget.
This item is from an album which has photographs relating to a number of families, including Boylans of Hilltown, Co. Louth, and Esmondes and Deane-Morgans of Co. Wexford.
Sweetman Album R.22416

Kenilworth Bowling Club, Grosvenor Square, Rathmines, Dublin. The club was founded in 1892 at premises in Kenilworth Square. In 1905 it moved to Grosvenor Square where this clubhouse was erected. The photograph probably dates from that year or shortly after. Ladies did not become members until the 1920s.

The flag used by the club at the time shows a lion rampant and a High Cross which were elements of the arms of the Borough of Rathmines and Rathgar.

Eason 1846

A Gaelic football match at O'Donnell Park, Letterkenny,
Co. Donegal, *c*.1950.
Valentine R.732

The rugby international, Ireland *v* England, at Lansdowne Road, Dublin, 13 February 1955. The result was a draw, 6 points each. *Ireland:* W.R. Tector, R. Roche, N.J. Henderson, A. O'Reilly, A.C. Pedlow, J.M. Kyle, A. O'Meara, F.E. Anderson, R. Roe, P. O'Donoghue, M.N. Madden, T.E. Reid, J.S. McCarthy (Capt.), R. Kavanagh, M.J. Cunningham.
Morgan 865

A group on an outing to Dalkey, Co. Dublin, *c.*1860. The
railway line from Dalkey to Bray was built in the early
1850s and the earth banked up to the left of the foot-bridge
looks relatively recent.
Stereo P.747A

Tourists and boatmen at Killarney, Co. Kerry, period
1860-80. Even at this early date Killarney already had a
considerable tourist trade.
Stereo P.146

The ladies bathing place, Portrush, Co. Antrim, *c.*1900. At this period Portrush was the most popular seaside resort in the North. At most resorts men and women bathed at separate beaches, a tradition that has survived up to the present time at some locations.
Lawrence R.2215

SLANE CASTLE. Co. MEATH. 9997 W.L.

The passenger steamer *Ros-na-Righ* on the Boyne passing
Slane Castle, Co. Meath, *c.*1905. The vessel made three
round trips a week up to Navan, starting at Oldbridge a
little above Drogheda.
Lawrence C.9997

Dancing on the road at Glendalough, Co. Wicklow, in the
late 1920s.
Valentine 96436

A day out at the Royal Dublin Society, Ballsbridge, in the 1920s.
Eason 1652

CLIFF ROAD, ENNISCRONE. VR.8499.

Day-trippers at Enniscrone, Co. Sligo, in the late 1940s. The village was then a busy seaside resort. The catchment area took in a large part of Co. Mayo including the town of Ballina, which accounts for the fact that the three motor car registrations which can be discerned (1Z) are from Co. Mayo.
Valentine R.8499

Punchestown Races, Co. Kildare, 27 April 1954. The *Irish Independent* described the occasion: 'Five thousand private cars packed with racegoers, more than fifty buses as well as innumerable cyclists and people on foot contributed yesterday to the life and movement generally associated with Punchestown on opening day.' On the day Paddy Sleator turned out three winners, Mountain Speck II, Venetian Law and Rushdale. The opening race was won by the fourteen-year-old Jim Cash.
Morgan 1